Neanderthal Conundrum: 34N; 117W
Copyrighted (2014) – David Paraiso
ISBN: 978-0-578-13793-3

Book Cover Description

This book is one piece of a larger puzzle in understanding the unraveling of a once highly esteemed and role model Diaspora in the 1960s thru 1980s, and proposing various options for its renaissance.

Contents of the book include: comparisons with other Diasporas and historical figures; insider observations: 1974-2014; factors 1 thru 18; elements of good governance; and, recommendations.

TABLE OF CONTENTS

Achievements: Awards, Beauty Contests, Cultural and Social Events 4
Objectives of the Book 5
Audiences of the book 5
Qualification and Disclaimer 5
What is the criteria for entries being included in the book? 7
What are the sources of the book? 7
What are the triggers for writing this book? 8
Insider Observations: 1974-2014 10
Factor 1 – Training of Leaders and Constituents 12
Factor 2 – The Damages Caused By Regionalism 16
Factor 3 – Standardization and Discipline 20
Factor 4 – Keeping an Open Mind: Stealth 117A Technology 20
Factor 5 – We Are Waiting to Be Invited; Tradition vs Adaptation 22
Factor 6 – Managing Differences and Conflicts 22
Factor 7 – Barkada System; "Adopting "best practices" or "best of all world models" 24
Factor 8 - Delicadeza 25
Factor 9 – Crab Mentality 25
Factor 10 – Money Clubs That Work on Trust 26
Factor 11 – Pooling Resources 27
Factor 12 - Size matters 27
Factor 13 – Long Term Strategy 28
Factor 14 - Protocols 29
Factor 15 – Investing in the Homeland (or, country of origin) 29
Factor 16 - Types of organizations sampled in this book 30
Factor 17 – Lack of Community Involvement 30

Factor 18 – Missed Opportunities	30
Promising Organizations in the Community	32
Elements of Good Governance	33
Recommendations	34
Questions	36
Attributes of the Diaspora	36
Additional References	38
Glossary and Terms	39
Attachment A – Gaps with Other Diasporas	40
Attachment B – Medical Practice	46
Attachment D – Music	49

Achievements: Awards, Beauty Contests, Cultural and Social Events

If one attends these events honoring the achievements of honorees in the Fil-Am Diaspora, one will conclude that this community is at the top of the food chain, and it is second to no one in this part of the world. There is one of these events almost every week somewhere in Southern California. But, is this an accurate conclusion?

Reply: between forty (1974s) to thirty (1980s) years ago, these were true if we are measuring the pecking order of various Diaspora communities in Attachment A – political, economic, professional/career advancement, trade and commerce, etc.

Reply: sadly, today in 2014, - not even close. The other Diasporas in Attachment A, have left the Fil-Am Diaspora behind.

This book is one piece of a larger puzzle in understanding the unraveling of a once highly esteemed and role model community, and presenting various options for its renaissance.

Objectives of the Book

1) This is a reference for the "Fil-Am Diaspora Renaissance" initiative focusing on the "current-state" comparison of the community with other Diasporas in the Southern California area and historical figures.
2) Serve as a trigger and catalyst for a vigorous and ongoing forum in understanding the gaps and challenges facing the community, and the options in remediating the gaps. Please refer to the following sections of the book:

    1. Elements of Good Governance
    2. Recommendations

3) Overcome the self-denial mentality that has been pervasive in the Diaspora.
4) Challenge various stakeholders inside and outside of the community, and create the conditions so we can work together in remediating the gaps of the community.

This is a "work in progress" document. We anticipate updating this book at least every 2 years.

In dissecting and presenting our observations and recommendations at this level, we are hoping that this will result in a series of robust and sustained activities from the community and its stakeholders.

Audiences of the book

1) Transplants
2) Next Generations
3) Hybrids
4) Researchers
5) Enthusiasts

Qualification and Disclaimer

The contents of this book are based on a list of insider observations taken in the Southern California area during the recent 40 years. From a clinical perspective analogy, this is the equivalent of conducting a biopsy of the community in order to trigger a renaissance.

What is the criteria for entries being included in the book?

1) It is a repetitive behavior or pattern across organizations and stakeholders.
2) It is systemic and structural in nature.
3) It is serious enough to be called out.
4) It is verifiable.

The entries in this book are not intended to be an exhaustive list of all the factors and parameters affecting the Diaspora. The approach taken is the equivalent of conducting a biopsy of the community and comparing the results with other communities.

What are the sources of the book?

The book contents are from insiders serving in various capacities at PriceWaterHouse (PwC), DeLoitte and Touche, Accenture, Kaiser Permanente, Cedar-Sinai, Bank of America, Wells Fargo, Bechtel, Fluor Corporation, WellPoint, Healthnet, international law firms, Los Angeles Times; UCLA, USC, UC-Irvine, UC-Riverside, Loyola Marymount University, SCPASA and other institutions; Chambers of commerce - Japanese, South Korean, Chinese, Vietnamese, Armenians, Fil-Ams, Blacks, Hispanics; APEX, LEAP, Greenlining Institute, and others.

The following contributed in finalizing this book:

1) Fred Antonio
2) Vicencio Godoyo
3) JLII
4) David Paraiso

JLII and David Paraiso have been friends since they were 4-year old toddlers. Fred Antonio, Vicencio Godoyo, JLII and David Paraiso have been colleagues and friends since the 1980s in Southern California.

Please send feedback and inquiries about the contents of this book to:

Neanderthal.Conundrum@gmail.com

From the perspective of Diaspora awakening and triggering a renaissance, the team hopes that this book could be a microcosm of **Harriet Beecher Stowe's Uncle Tom's Cabin published in 1852.**

http://en.wikipedia.org/wiki/Uncle_Tom's_Cabin

Uncle Tom's Cabin; or, Life Among the Lowly, is an anti-slavery novel by American author Harriet Beecher Stowe. Published in 1852, the novel "helped lay the groundwork for the Civil War", according to Will Kaufman.

Stowe, a Connecticut-born teacher at the Hartford Female Academy and an active abolitionist, featured the character of Uncle Tom, a long-suffering black slave around whom the stories of other characters revolve. The sentimental novel depicts the reality of slavery while also asserting that Christian love can overcome something as destructive as enslavement of fellow human beings.

Uncle Tom's Cabin was the best-selling novel of the 19th century and the second best-selling book of that century, following the Bible. It is credited with helping fuel the abolitionist cause in the 1850s. In the first year after it was published, 300,000 copies of the book were sold in the United States; one million copies were sold in Great Britain. In 1855, three years after it was published, it was called "the most popular novel of our day." The impact attributed to the book is great, reinforced by a story that when Abraham Lincoln met Stowe at the start of the Civil War, Lincoln declared, "So this is the little lady who started this great war. "The quote is apocryphal; it did not appear in print until 1896, and it has been argued that "The long-term durability of Lincoln's greeting as an anecdote in literary studies and Stowe scholarship can perhaps be explained in part by the desire among many contemporary intellectuals ... to affirm the role of literature as an agent of social change."

What are the triggers for writing this book?

1) Incidents involving several of my peers in the medical community and concerns about the self-inflicted and escalating marginalization of the community. Please refer to Observations: 1974-2014 Section of this book.
2) The global financial meltdown in 2008-2009 has exacerbated the situation in the community, particularly in Fil-Am local graduates capturing jobs.

3) Realization that the gaps we have been observing are systemic, across the board and getting worse.
4) Request for inputs from our peers and counterparts in Northern California, New York, New Jersey, Connecticut, Washington, Oregon, Texas, Illinois, Indiana, Virginia, Maryland, Washington D.C., West Virginia, Tennessee, Arizona, Nevada, Georgia, Hawaii, New England states, Mid-West states, Toronto, Vancouver, Ireland, England, Australia, Italy, France, South Korea, Tokyo-Japan, Hong kong, Taiwan, Malaysia, Singapore, the Middle East, and others. Please refer to:

http://en.wikipedia.org/wiki/Little_Manila

We believe that this book will spawn various discussions and activities which will contribute to the renaissance of the community.

Insider Observations: 1974-2014

The lack of cohesion and effective governance, have been hurting the Fil-Am community in Southern California in the following manner:

1) Fil-Am Skilled Nursing Facilities (SNFs) and medical practices are being taken over by groups from other communities which are better organized, with stronger political ties, and more effective governance.
2) Fil-Am medical practitioners are being marginalized in various facilities – LA County Jail, LA Sheriff, etc.
3) Compared to the Hispanics, Japanese, Koreans, Vietnamese, Chinese, Indians, Armenians and other communities, the next generation Fil-Am local graduates and students are not properly and effectively supported. As Mentoring Director at UCLA-PA Alumni and various organizations, I observed through the years the diminishing number of Fil-Am local graduates capturing 1st and 2 tier positions in 1 and 2nd tier companies; this has been the trend during the recent 40 years. Please note that there are families and individuals who are very successful in their careers and endeavors. But these they achieved mostly on their own, and not attributable and traceable to community support.
4) When the alumni of other communities meet, they meet at the board rooms of Bank of America, Wells Fargo, PriceWaterHouse, multi-national law firms and corporations with pre-arranged parking. When Fil-Am alumni meet, they meet at local restaurants where they can hardly hear each other, parking is a nightmare and their cars vandalized.
5) When the local students of other communities need scholarships and funding, they tap the resources of Bank of America, Wells Fargo, PriceWaterHouse, prestigious law firms and global corporations like Samsung, Hyundai, Toyota, Ford, GM, etc... When Fil-Am students need scholarship and funding, they solicit from Goldilock, local stores, local restaurants and retired Fil-Ams.
6) When a Fil-Am organization receives several million dollars in grants, the community jumps up and down. Just drive 7 miles East of Los Angeles, the Hispanic community delivers billions of dollars' worth of grants and programs into their communities, and with political appointments and clout that go along with them. The same applies to the Black, South Korean, Vietnamese and other communities. These organizations have access to resources that they can invite hundreds and thousands with free steak lunch/dinner and entertainments.

7) Elected officials determine how much of our federal, state, county and city tax dollars go back to the community. Since we have very few at these levels, if any, our community is not a priority when it comes funding and political appointments.
8) The Hispanics, Japanese, Chinese, South Koreans, Vietnamese, Indians and Armenians are in their 2 or 3rd generation political presence and continuity in their respective jurisdictions. Fil-Ams don't have any at the state and federal levels. Occasionally, there will be Fil-Ams at the city levels, but they do not last that long. It takes about 20 years to recruit, train and nurture a successful elected officials – starting from the local board, then the city council, then county, then state, then federal.
9) After 20 or more years in the U.S. - Hispanic, Japanese, Chinese, South Korean, Vietnamese, Indian and Armenian medical groups and practitioners, operate chains of medical practices in both the U.S. and their countries of origin. Fil-Ams do not have a track record on this, and when they do, it was taken over by the Thais – like the Asean Hospital in Alabang.
10) During the board meetings of several Fil-Am professional and trade organizations, I asked why they have not been proactive politically in the same manner as the Hispanics, Chinese, Vietnamese, Koreans and others. I was told officially, that they are waiting to be invited.
11) The Fil-Am community is in a state of denial on these issues. The community has been spending more resources in awards, beauty contests, dinner dances and other social events.
12) The other communities have such enormous clout that they are able to nominate, position and nurture interns from their communities at the Office of the Governor of the State of California, and other key elected officials at the state, county, and federal levels. The also do this with several Fortune 500 and multi-nationals. We did not find any evidence of Fil-Ams matching this level of influence.
13) Consequences of these trends: (1) remittance to the Philippines; (2) marginalization of the community – politically, economically, professionally, etc.; (3) failure to invest in the Philippines will haunt us – there is no homeland to go back to.

As Fil-Am businesses lose ground to other groups, our professionals being marginalized, and the earlier generations retire, remittance to the Philippines will collapse. According to our sources, at least 60% of dollar remittance to the Philippines are originating from North America, and a big chunk of this is from the Fil-Am medical community.

Factor 1 – Training of Leaders and Constituents

In various cultures, part of the training of leaders and constituents at an early age is in living through and managing highly stressful and uncomfortable situations. The trainees are required to knock at doors and/or approach people of other communities, and introduce products and services. This is the equivalent of the young Mormons working in pairs to various communities to proselytize, except that the trainees in this case are not paired with anybody.

Most Fil-Ams are not trained in this manner. The consequences are: (1) Fil-Ams are unable to operate effectively outside of their "comfort zone", and when exposed to it, they lose objectivity, and miss opportunities for themselves and the community; (2) they adapt a "balat sibuyas" mentality which makes them too sensitive when criticism occurs or alternatives to their ideas are presented – these are disastrous and serious liabilities when performing leadership and advisory functions; (3) these breed of leaders and constituents tend to bring in like-minded individuals, which turns off the most promising and capable members of the community; (4) with the most promising and capable members of the community gone, and with leaders and constituents operating without guidance, proper checks and balances, everything goes downhill from that point on. This is one of the primary reasons why the community stagnated and unraveled during the recent 4 decades.

Fil-Ams with the mentality of being a king in a small island rather than a stakeholder in a bigger community, spawn at least 3 problems. FIRST, this is a deterrent in the formation of larger structures and collaboration to compete effectively against the other Diasporas and juggernauts; SECOND, if this group is the primary source of leaders and constituents for the community, they do not have the corporate and mainstream across the board collaborative experience and proficiencies to effectively govern; THIRD, this is a turn-off for the more promising and capable members who are usually integrated with the mainstream and other communities. This creates a second tier in the Diaspora, where the more promising and capable members are in-absentia in key community activities. The two tiers do not mix. One can easily detect the proficiency and experience gaps in meetings and projects in federal, state, county, city or corporate settings. These gaps have negative long-term consequences for the community.

Parable: The Story of the Chicken and the Hen - A story about belief and expectation

http://takelight.wordpress.com/2013/11/06/the-story-of-the-chicken-and-the-hen-a-story-about-belief-and-expectation/

'Once upon a time a man found an eagle's egg and placed it under a brooding hen. The eaglet hatched with the chickens and grew to be like them. He clucked and cackled; scratched the earth for worms; flapped his wings and managed to a few feet in the air.

Years passed. One day, the eagle, now grown old, saw a magnificent bird above him in the sky. It glided in graceful majesty against the powerful wind, with scarcely a movement of its golden wings.

Spellbound, the eagle asked, "Who's that?"

"That's the king of the birds, the eagle, "said his neighbor. "He belongs to the sky. We belong to earth—we're chickens."

So the eagle lived and a chicken for that's what he thought he was.'

Parable: Little Frog in the Well

http://www.taiwandc.org/folk-fro.htm

My good friends, imagine if you were to live at the bottom of a deep, dark well. What kind of world would you see?

There was a Little Frog who lived at the bottom of a deep, dark well. Now let us go down there and see what kind of world he had.

It was a very old well filled with shallow water at the bottom. The walls of the well were all covered with wet moss. When the Little Frog was thirsty, he drank a little bit of the well water, and when he was hungry, he ate some insects. When he was tired, he lay on a little rock at the bottom of the well and looked up at the sky above him. Sometimes he saw passing clouds. He was very happy and satisfied.

Now, the Little Frog had been living at the bottom of this old well since he was born. He had never been to the outside world. Whenever a bird or birds flew by and stopped at the edge of the well, the Little Frog always looked up and bragged, "Hello! why don't you come down here and play with me. It's so pleasant down here. Look, I have cool water to drink and countless insects to eat. Come down! At night I can watch the twinkling stars, and sometimes I can see the beautiful moon, too."

Sometimes the birds would tell the Little Frog, "Hi, Little Frog! You see, the outside world is much bigger and nicer. It's many times more beautiful than your little well at the bottom. " But the Little Frog would not believe them. "Don't lie to me, I don't believe there is any place that could be better than here. "

Gradually, all the birds began to dislike him They thought he was too stubborn and stopped talking to him.

The Little Frog could not understand why nobody would like to come down to his nice place.

One day, a yellow sparrow stopped by at the edge of the well. The Little Frog was so excited he greeted the sparrow and invited the sparrow eagerly. "Hello, Mr. Yellow Sparrow, how are you? Please come down to my most beautiful house." The yellow sparrow did not say a word and flew away. The next day the yellow sparrow came again and the same thing happened again. It went on for six days. On the seventh day, the yellow sparrow finally said, "Little Frog, may I show you the outside world?" But the Little Frog refused the offer.

Finally the yellow sparrow became angry. He flew down to the bottom of the well, picked up the Little Frog on his back, and flew out of the well.

"Oh!" the Little Frog exclaimed. "How is it that the outside world is so big!" He had been in the bottom of his dark well for so long that the bright sunshine made his eyes blink shut, and he could hardly open his eyes to see.

When he finally opened his eyes, he saw so many things around him. "Hey! Be careful! Don't hit this strange thing. What are all these green high and low things?" The yellow sparrow laughed happily: "Ha! ha! These are mountains and valleys. There are countless mountains in this world. The Himalayas, the Swiss Alps, the Rockies and... "

The Little Frog could not believe there were so many big mountains in the world. When they flew over the high mountains, the next view made the Little Frog even more surprised.

"What is this long, silvery, shiny view?"

"It is a river," the yellow sparrow replied.

"Then what is that huge, blue thing over there?"

"That is a sea," the yellow sparrow replied.

"That river and sea, how much water do they have? How much bigger are they than my well? They must hold a billion times more water than my well." The Little Frog began to realize how tiny his well was. "Let's go down, O.K. ?" The yellow sparrow put the Little Frog down on the ground and flew away.

The Little Frog jumped into the grass and saw many beautiful flowers of different colors. He had never seen such beautiful flowers and had never smelled such nice scents. He kept on going and went into a forest. In it he looked up and saw many tall trees. He looked down and found many different kinds of fruits that had fallen to the ground. He picked up an apple and tasted it. "Wow, so sweet !" Then he listened to the beautiful singing of the birds. The cute squirrels were jumping, the monkeys were swinging from branch to branch, and the antelopes were scampering speedily.

In the pond, the lotus flowers were dancing in the air, and the lotus leaves were floating on the water like umbrellas. There were many fish in the water.

"The outside world is so big, so wonderful, and beautiful!" The Little Frog finally cried out happily and jumped into the pond. He climbed up on a huge lotus leaf and enjoyed his new life there. The yellow sparrow came back and asked, "Little Frog! How's this outside world? Big? Beautiful?"

"Thank you very much. If you had not brought me out to see this world, I would never had known that there are such beautiful things that exist outside my well ." The Little Frog never tried to go back to his old well again.

Factor 2 - The Damages Caused By Regionalism

During the American struggle for independence, to the consternation of his fellow Puritan New Englanders, John Adams nominated George Washington to lead the continental army and Thomas Jefferson to draft the Declaration of Independence - both of whom were from the slave-owning and tobacco growing state of Virginia. This is one example of how the founding fathers value merit and put the national interest more than regional affiliation. We have not identified the equivalent of this gesture in the Fil-Am community.

The Fil-Am behavior that we observed, "Transplant", "Next generations" and "Hybrid", is exclusionary and the equivalent of biological inbreeding which limits the talent pool, damages the DNA of what remains, and deters participation from the more forward looking and capable members of the community for generations. Forward looking and capable communities encourages outreach, diversity and taking risks. Using a fruit growing scenario, these cultures facilitate diversity via grafting and pruning as a standard practice. Fil-Am culture is focused in replicating models that worked a long time ago, but are no longer relevant in today's setting.

The Fil-Am culture that we observed is like sand – it holds very little moisture and nutrients needed by plants to grow and thrive. Whatever one puts into sand quickly evaporates. The only thing that grows in sand is cactus. On the other hand, forward looking and capable cultures are like humus soil or clay – they create conditions that retain moisture and nutrients which can support a variety of flora and fauna.

Let me illustrate an example of the "cactus" scenario. In Los Angeles County, we have the following public TV stations: Vietnamese – 10; Korean - 5; Chinese - 7; Hispanics – 5; Armenians -2; Filipinos – 1 (part time and shared). The Historic Filipino town is not a match with Little Saigon in Westminster, Little Tokyo in LA, China Town in Monterey Park/Alhambra, Armenia Town in Glendale, and other communities. The only remaining Fil-Am bank in Los Angeles is for remittance purposes only, while the other communities are teeming with international and global banks focusing on trade and commerce.

Regionalism in the Fil-Am Diaspora is feudalism in a different form. Feudalism's decline and the ascendancy of National Identity in other Diasporas were triggered by the Meiji Restoration in the case of Japan, and the Crusades in the case of Western Europe. No such event or equivalent ever happened in the Fil-Am Diaspora, or the homeland.

Meiji Restoration in Japan

http://en.wikipedia.org/wiki/Meiji_Restoration

How did the crusades affect the feudal system?

http://www.lordsandladies.org/effects-of-crusades.htm

Reversing the impact of regionalism is not trivial and will take some time. After all, we are all creatures of habit and we tend to replicate the models that we are exposed to.

Parable: The Daffodil

http://www.bankofideas.com.au/Stories/fables.html

Several times my daughter had telephoned to say, "Mother, you must come see the daffodils before they are over." I wanted to go, but it was a two-hour drive from Laguna to Lake Arrowhead. "I will come next Tuesday," I promised, a little reluctantly, on her third call. Next Tuesday dawned cold and rainy. Still, I had promised, and so I drove there. When I finally walked into Carolyn's house and hugged and greeted my grandchildren, I said, "Forget the daffodils, Carolyn! The road is invisible in the clouds and fog, and there is nothing in the world except you and these children that I want to see bad enough to drive another inch!" My daughter smiled calmly and said, "We drive in this all the time, Mother." "Well, you won't get me back on the road until it clears, and then I'm heading for home!" I assured her.

"I was hoping you'd take me over to the garage to pick up my car." "How far will we have to drive?" "Just a few blocks," Carolyn said. "I'll drive. I'm used to this." After several minutes, I had to ask, "Where are we going? This isn't the way to the garage!" "We're going to my garage the long way," Carolyn smiled, "by way of the daffodils." "Carolyn," I said sternly, "please turn around." "It's all right, Mother, I promise. You will never forgive yourself if you miss this experience." After about twenty minutes, we turned onto a small gravel road and I saw a small church. On the far side of the church, I saw a hand-lettered sign that read, "Daffodil Garden." We got out of the car and each took a child's hand, and I followed Carolyn down the path. Then, we turned a corner of the path, and I looked up and gasped. Before me lay the most glorious sight. It looked as though someone had taken a great vat of gold and poured it down over the mountain peak and slopes. The flowers were planted in majestic, swirling patterns- great ribbons and swaths of deep orange, white, lemon, yellow, salmon pink, saffron, and butter yellow. Each different-colored Variety Was planted as a group so that it swirled and flowed like its own River With its own unique hue. * There were five acres of flowers. "But who has done this?" I Asked Carolyn.

"It's just one woman," Carolyn answered. "She lives on the Property. That's her home." Carolyn pointed to a well kept a frame house That Looked small and modest in the midst of all that glory. We walked up to The House. On the patio, we saw a poster. "Answers to the Questions I Know You are asking" was the headline. The first answer was a simple one."50,000 bulbs," it read. The Second Answer was, "One at a time, by one woman. Two hands, two feet, and very Little brain." The third answer was, "Began in 1958." There it was, The Daffodil Principle. For me, that moment was a Life-changing experience.

I thought of this woman whom I had never met, who, more than Forty years before, had begun-one bulb at a time-to bring her vision of Beauty and Joy to an obscure mountain top. Still, just planting one bulb at A Time, Year after year, had changed the world. This unknown woman had Forever Changed the world in which she lived. She had created something Of Ineffable (Indescribable) magnificence, beauty, and inspiration.

The principle her daffodil garden taught is one of the greatest Principles Of celebration. That is, learning to move toward our goals and Desires One Step at a time-often just one baby-step at a time-and learning to Love The Doing, learning to use the accumulation of time. When we multiply tiny pieces of time with small increments of daily effort, we too will find we can accomplish magnificent things. We can change the world.

"It makes me sad in a way," I admitted to Carolyn. "What might I have accomplished if I had thought of a wonderful goal thirty-five or forty years ago and had worked away at it 'one bulb at a time' through all those years.

Just think what I might have been able to achieve!"

My daughter summed up the message of the day in her usual direct Way. "Start tomorrow," she said.

It's so pointless to think of the lost hours of yesterdays. The way to make learning a lesson of celebration instead of a cause for regret is to only ask, "How can I put this to use today?"

Author Unknown

Factor 3 – Standardization and Discipline

Successful Diasporas in Attachment A value the strategic and economic benefits of standardization and discipline. The Fil-Am Diaspora has yet to learn this.

- Successful companies and communities are motivated to participate in standardization because they gain an edge over non-participating companies and communities in terms of insider knowledge. Early access to information is valuable.
- "Standardization eventually lead to lower transaction costs in the economy as a whole, as well as to savings for individual businesses and communities."
- "Cooperation between companies and communities in matters of standardization is advantageous since the resulting synergy can help reduce costs and increase profits."
- "Businesses and communities not only reduce the economic risk of their R&D activities by participating in standardization, but can also lower their R&D costs."

Factor 4 – Keeping an Open Mind: Stealth 117A Technology

In 1964, Pyotr Ufimtsev, a Soviet mathematician, published a seminal paper titled Method of Edge Waves in the Physical Theory of Diffraction in the journal of the Moscow Institute for Radio Engineering. In the 1970s, Lockheed analyst Denys Overholser found Ufimtsev's paper, and used the formula in the development of the Lockheed F-117 Nighthawk.

The F-117 was widely publicized for its role in the Persian Gulf War of 1991. It was commonly referred to as the "Stealth Fighter", although it was a strictly ground-attack aircraft. The Air Force retired the F-117 on 22 April 2008, primarily because of the fielding of the F-22 Raptor and the impending introduction of the multirole F-35 Lightning II.

The Fil-Am culture does not provide the type of open mindedness in learning and adopting the "best of all world practices" from various sources.

The Bill Gates and Steve Jobs achievements would not have thrived in a Fil-Am culture. Their achievements require constructive and sustained "copetition", meaning collaborate and compete concurrently for the benefit of all. The Fil-Am culture is the equivalent of clubbing each other into oblivion, and is very destructive across generations.

Presidents like Bill Clinton or Barack Obama will not have a chance in a Fil-Am culture.

An academic "Transplant" from the Philippines was approached by investors from Southern California, and the first question he asked is – how many books have you written? This mindset partly explains why there are hardly any processed and competitive products and services from the Fil-Am Diaspora.

References:

Lockheed F-117 Nighthawk

http://en.wikipedia.org/wiki/Lockheed_F-117_Nighthawk

Japanese Learning Gospel Music

http://www.scpr.org/programs/take-two/2014/02/11/35977/japanese-students-wow-la-churches-with-gospel-musi/

http://www.scpr.org/programs/take-two/2014/02/06/35916/sister-act-2-inspires-japanese-students-to-sing-go/

South Koreans Learning Talmud

http://www.aish.com/jw/s/South_Koreans_Learning_Talmud.html

Chinese Interest on the Talmud

http://www.huffingtonpost.com/michael-levy/the-rise-of-the-chinese-y_b_812462.html

Some Georgia Schools Make Mandarin Mandatory

http://www.npr.org/2012/09/08/160028396/looking-to-future-ga-schools-require-mandarin

$300 Million Scholarship for Study in China Signals a New Focus

http://www.nytimes.com/2013/04/21/world/asia/us-financier-backs-china-scholarship-program.html?src=me&ref=general&_r=0

Factor 5 – We Are Waiting to Be Invited; Tradition vs Adaptation

During the board meetings of several the Fil-Am professional and trade organizations, we asked why they have not been proactive politically in the same manner as the Hispanics, Chinese, Vietnamese, Koreans and others have been. We were told, that they are waiting to be invited. This is an elitist and anachronistic mentality that leads to marginalization and extinction in the U.S.

Most of the community leaders and constituents that we sampled are predisposed and more focused in preserving homeland tradition rather than mastering and adopting the "best practices" or "best of all world models" from various Diasporas and the corporate world. As a result, the model Diaspora of the 70s and 80s missed the boat.

Factor 6 – Managing Differences and Conflicts

One enabler or disabler of a community is how differences and conflicts are managed.

In the case of Kennedy vs Nixon (1960 election) and Bush vs Gore (2000 election), the losing candidates (Nixon and Gore), declined to mount a challenge for the sake of the country. We do not know of any equivalent gestures like this in the Fil-Am Diaspora. The records that we had access to indicate, persistent internal strife and the community sadly fragmented.

For specifics, please refer to:

Kennedy vs Nixon

http://www.slate.com/articles/news_and_politics/history_lesson/2000/10/was_nixon_robbed.html

Bush vs Gore

http://www.digitalhistory.uh.edu/disp_textbook.cfm?smtID=2&psid=3377

FACLA Scandal in Los Angeles

http://www.pinoywatchdog.com/it%E2%80%99s-time-to-end-the-facla-%E2%80%9Ccurse%E2%80%9D/

Rose Parade Scandal in Pasadena

http://www.mabuhayradio.com/op-ed-page/today-is-the-14th-anniversary-of-the-philippine-scandal-at-the-pasadena-tournament-of-roses

Kalayaan beauty contest marred by ugly accusations

http://thefilam.net/archives/10856

Antonio Luna Assassination

http://en.wikipedia.org/wiki/Antonio_Luna

Andres Bonifacio Assassination

http://en.wikipedia.org/wiki/Andr%C3%A9s_Bonifacio

Factor 7 – Barkada System; "Adopting "best practices" or "best of all world models"

A "Next-Generation" Vietnamese Chairman of one of the leading Asian organization in Southern California approached me to train his Board of Directors and Officers in acquiring and mastering the basic and advanced skills in corporate governance. We do not know of any Fil-Am organization reaching out and making this type of outreach. The prevailing mentality is that Fil-Ams know what they are doing, and they need NO assistance from anybody.

At the other end of the spectrum, as Director of Mentoring for a Fil-Am alumni group and 1-1/2 years of preparations, I brought in senior and hiring managers from Fortune 500 and multi-national companies to enhance the career prospects of Fil-Am alumni from this highly regarded and esteemed institution only to be ambushed by the "Barkada" elements of the organization. They would rather seek their job leads and mentoring from fellow barkadas who graduated years earlier (but with minimal experience, influence and contacts), rather than the Senior Partners or high level VPs or Directors of multi-billion dollar global companies. All invitations extended to this group that could lead to long-term career opportunities with these Fortune 500 and multi-national companies resulted in "no shows" among Fil-Ams but a high level of enthusiastic and sustained participation from the Chinese, Japanese, Koreans, Vietnamese, and others. This partly explains why the decreasing number of Fil-Ams are being hired by 1st and 2nd tier companies during the last 4 decades, and why the Fil-Am alumni are meeting in noisy restaurants, while the alumni of the other communities are meeting at the board rooms (with secured parking) of Bank of America, Wells Fargo and other global companies. The "balat sibuyas" syndrome is definitely at play here because the Fil-Am alumni do not feel comfortable engaging Senior Partners or high level VPs or Directors of multi-billion dollar global companies.

Briefly, these examples accentuate behavior that definitely was a factor in the Diaspora falling behind.

Factor 8 - Delicadeza

The community is severely lacking on this – this is true for the "Transplants", "The Next Generations" and "Hybrids".

Fil-Am organizations and Fil-Ams will publicly club each into oblivion, and not sensitive to the long-term impact to them, the community and their supporters. This is probably related to the lack of "national identity". Members of other communities are more sensitive engaging in deeds that could result in the entire community being judged negatively.

Examples of this are the Rose Parade and FACLA scandals; UCLA Tail Gate, Kaiser Permanente, Kaplan, Filipino Caucus United Methodist Church, and other incidents.

Another example is physicians bringing in non-physician spouses during CMEs. Several of the biggest players in the pharmaceutical industry take exception to this behavior of Fil-Am physicians.

Factor 9 – Crab Mentality

I was one of the speakers at an International Technology conference in Long Beach in 2004 and a NAFAA Conference in Hawaii in 2006. In both instances, we were promoting the Philippines.

Guess who publicly ambushed us during both conferences? You are correct if you answered they were Filipinos and Fil-Ams. The non Fil-Am audiences defended us during the events.

There is a consistent pattern in the community that is resentful of a Filipino or a Fil-Am getting attention. In other cultures, the reverse is true.

> **Divisiveness among Fil-Ams**
>
> http://denganda.wordpress.com/tag/fil-am-community/
>
> http://www.bakitwhy.com/bwc/blogs/stevenraga/broken-system-fil-am-student-leadership-development-northeast-part-i-role

Mrs. Kalayaan beauty contest marred by ugly accusations

http://thefilam.net/archives/10856

Emelita Breyer Discrimination Case

http://www.mabuhayradio.com/civil-rights/another-summary-of-the-breyer-discrimination-case-and-progress-report

Factor 10 – Money Clubs That Work on Trust

http://articles.philly.com/2003-11-17/news/25462326_1_immigrants-payout-money

At 7 p.m. in the South Philadelphia rowhouse, friends and relatives, many of them entrepreneurs, stopped chatting and pulled up chairs. Each had been paying $500 a month into a 28-month, 28-member hui, or loan "share" club. Time had come for the monthly payout.

In the club, each person commits to giving a certain amount of money every month until 28 months have passed. Each month, one person walks home from the meeting with all that money and cash. But then that person has to keep paying back for the next 27 months until all of his or her friends in the group have gotten their pot of money. This work on positive peer pressure and is very powerful.

"Members get money to buy a business or buy a store . . . or pay for a wedding, or anything. "Members don't like banks; they ask a lot of questions."

For immigrant entrepreneurs, money-pooling clubs such as the hui help form an arsenal for survival and advantage. Along with tireless labor, unpaid help from relatives, family lenders, and patronage from their own ethnic community, immigrants can leverage resources in ways that native-born capitalists cannot. Many ethnic groups have their own loan clubs. The Ethiopian version is ekub, Jamaican is partners, Dominican san, Korean keh and Cambodian tong-tine.

Trust at the level of the other communities does not exist in the Fil-Am Diaspora, particularly across regions. The consequences are: (1) without sufficient financial resources, progress within the community is muted –

politically, economically, professionally, etc.; (2) this means that major opportunities are lost; (3) when the more forward looking and capable members of the community see this, they avoid the community, exacerbating the situation.

In today's global economy, larger, more organized and effective communities can bring down a bigger prey. This could not be said of the Fil-Am Diaspora which could only bring down the smallest and the least desirable and left-over of prey.

Factor 11 – Pooling Resources

Many immigrants get an edge simply by pooling their efforts. The Korean Grocers Association strikes deals with food suppliers - Pepsi, Coke, Tastykake, Herr's - to provide discounts to its exclusively Korean members. "We make deals for better prices," said David Kim, a director of the association of about 500 members around Philadelphia.

Immigrant family members create a strong social support system for one another, pooling resources to start businesses and buy homes, providing a safety net if someone falls on hard times, and helping each another integrate into our communities.

Trust at the level of the other communities does not exist in the Fil-Am Diaspora, particularly across regions. The consequences are: (1) pooling of resources seldom occur, and if they do occur, this occur on a small-scale basis; (2) this means that major opportunities are lost; (3) when the more forward looking and capable members of the community see this, they avoid the community, exacerbating the situation.

Factor 12 - Size matters

Imagine if the Union forces under President Abraham Lincoln lost the civil war during 1861-1865? The United States as we know it today, would have been reduced to nimbler and less effective countries; this is the equivalent of the Fil-Am Diaspora fragmenting into "self-inflicted" marginalized pieces that we know of today.

Who would have rescued Europe and other countries (including the

Philippines) in World War I and II? There is no other country progressive, capable and big enough to turn the tide of history.

Though Filipinos is the largest group listed in Attachment A, regionalism, constant infighting, fragmentation and weak governance have reduced the Fil-Am Diaspora to the lower tiers – in politics, trade and commerce, choicest jobs and professional careers, and other types of empowerment.

One can easily detect the pattern and predisposition to fragment within the Fil-Am Diaspora. During elections, when one candidate loses, the losing candidate forms a separate organization so he/she can be elected, and if he/she is not elected, he/she forms yet another organization until he/she is elected. As an example, the "Kalayaan-Philippine Independence" celebration, there is a pattern of multiple Fil-Am organizations conducting the same event at the same time in the same city (sometimes in adjacent rooms or buildings) across the U.S. This is a big turn-off for the next generation and outsiders, and degraded the community to being a laughing stock of other communities, and the mainstream.

Some Fil-Ams will argue, that they don't need to engage the community because they blend well with the mainstream. This is probably true provided one cannot detect the difference between them and the mainstream – in terms of appearance and behavior.

Another example - in various mailings lists, facebook and blog discussion groups via the internet, Fil-Am groups are several hundred members at maximum, most are below 100 members with constant flaming or toxic messages being lodged against each other. Compare these with those from the Chinese, Indian, Indonesian communities of 200,000 or more mostly well behaved members...

Factor 13 – Long Term Strategy

Fred and I have been discussing the long-term career prospect of his son, Kevin - a medical doctor and a graduate of UC-San Diego.

Kevin is extremely good in what he does and we have no doubt that in at least 10 years, he would qualify as a Medical Director for the San Diego County Health System or UC-San Diego Medical Center, or equivalent institutions. However, he probably will not get the job because the other ethnic communities are better connected – politically, economically and academically with key stakeholders.

The Fil-Am Diaspora does not have a strategy at the local, county, state or federal levels. If one exists, it is probably disjointed. The consequences are: (1) progress within the community is muted – politically, economically, professionally, etc.; (2) this means that major opportunities are lost; (3) when the more forward looking and capable members of the community see this, they avoid the community, exacerbating the situation.

In other communities, we documented their "Next Generations" working for Global Investment and Traditional Banks during daytime, and performing custodian functions by nighttime in their respective communities. They draw their leaders and key constituents from this group. We have no known equivalents of this in the Fil-Am Diaspora.

Factor 14 - Protocols

In the early 2000s, there was a time when the Philippine Consulate in Los Angeles did not have a website. So as part of my outreach and for almost 2 years, I volunteered and paid for the Philippine Consulate website from my own pocket. I found out later that another party was publicly claiming to be the one subsidizing the website without my knowledge and consent.

Factor 15 – Investing in the Homeland (or, country of origin)

After 20 or more years in the U.S. - Hispanic, Japanese, Chinese, South Korean, Vietnamese, Indian and Armenian professionals operate chains of businesses in both the U.S. and their countries of origin. Fil-Ams do not have a track record on this.

For thousands of years, Jews and other Diasporas knew the need for a homeland where they could return to. Fil-Ams have yet to learn this lesson. The Fil-Am Diaspora will pay a high price for not making this investment, particularly when they lose traditional family bond due to being anglicized.

Factor 16 - Types of organizations sampled in this book

1) Corporate
2) Professional
3) Trade groups (chambers of commerce, press club, accounting, etc.)
4) Community (church, non-profits)
5) Cultural
6) Social

Most of these organizations are being administered and operated as social and cultural organizations. We believe that this is the case because the forward-looking, experienced and proficient leaders and constituents with corporate and mainstream backgrounds are mostly not participating in these organizations. The effectiveness of organizations is directly proportional to the acumen, proficiencies and connection/network of the leaders and constituents.

Factor 17 – Lack of Community Involvement

Most members of the Diaspora are not community minded, or their community involvement are limited to the church, social and cultural functions. The "Next Generations" grow up in this environment, and they replicate the model to the detriment of the community.

Factor 18 – Missed Opportunities

Due to the previous 17 factors enumerated above, the community lost a lot of opportunities. Two examples are:

1) **Larry Itlong and Cesar Chavez**

   http://www.nytimes.com/2012/10/19/us/larry-itliong-forgotten-filipino-labor-leader.html?_r=0

   http://en.wikipedia.org/wiki/Cesar_Chavez

2) **UCLA Alumni Incident**

Promising Organizations in the Community

There are 2 promising models in rebuilding the Diaspora. They need our support and attention.

ISFFA

    http://www.isffa.org/

UCLA PCH

    http://pchatucla.weebly.com/

    https://www.facebook.com/pages/Pre-Health-Students-Organizations-United-PUSOUCI-PCHUCLA-FIHSUCR/119726291121

Elements of Good Governance

1) Diaspora identity. We have none.
2) Comprehensive strategy and plan. We have none.
3) Comprehensive training program and support system for leaders and constituents. We have none.
4) Forward-looking, experienced, proficient and well-connected leaders. A good number of our leaders do not have corporate training or exposure, and do not feel comfortable operating in a corporate setting. As such, they govern and manage projects as social and cultural events - abundant in symbolisms like picture taking, management by decrees, dropping names, awards, etc.
5) Intelligent and engaged constituents. Most constituents do not vote based on issues or merit; they vote along family and regional lines.
6) Operational bureaucracy. This is mostly personality-based within the Diaspora; chaos is the norm. Other communities have bureaucracies that will keep running regardless of who is in charge.
7) Checks and balances. We have none.
8) Standardization/Discipline. We have none.
9) Trust. We have none.
10) Unity and ongoing support. We have none.
11) Resources. Very limited because there is no trust and credibility within the community. Due to lack of elected official representation at the federal, state, state and local levels, allocation of funds and appointments for the community are at the lower tiers of the waiting queues.

In a scale of 0-10, 0 being the lowest, 10 being the highest rating among the 11 parameters above, the Fil-Am Diaspora is not competitive with the other Diasporas in Attachment A. We believe that this is the case because the forward-looking, experienced and proficient leaders and constituents with corporate and mainstream backgrounds are mostly not participating in the organizations that we sampled.

Recommendations

1) Conduct an ongoing forum on this subject with the right stakeholders.
2) Based on the "best practices" identified in this book, develop and update training programs for both the leaders and constituents. Focus on key proficiencies, and measure progress over time. This should include the family, church, schools, etc.
3) Address the gaps identified in this book - strategy, mentoring, etc.
4) Develop and roll out programs that will attract the best and the brightest; train, nurture, incubate, support and keep them.
5) Concentrate in areas so we can elect our own candidates; concentrate resources instead of spreading out thin.
6) Forge alliances with various political, economic stakeholders within and outside of the community; understand their needs and support them on those needs.
7) Learn and adopt "best practices" or "best of all world models" from other Diasporas and the corporate world. This means reaching out and learning from the other Diasporas and juggernauts.
8) Develop and implement programs that will build trust and collaboration.
9) Develop and implement programs that promote patriotic or national identity including watching movies like the **7 Samurais and Farewell My Concubine**

http://en.wikipedia.org/wiki/Seven_Samurai

http://en.wikipedia.org/wiki/Farewell_My_Concubine_(film)

10) Develop and implement programs that will keep the "Transplants", "Next Generations", and "Hybrids" connected with the homeland.
11) Vigorously invest in the rebuilding of the homeland. Starting reference materials for this are:

Rewilding

http://www.ted.com/talks/george_monbiot_for_more_wonder_rewild_the_world.html

http://www.npr.org/2013/09/27/225426662/can-rewilding-restore-vanishing-ecosystems

12) Continue conducting research on this subject and update this book.
13) Where appropriate and practical, collaborate with Filipinos or ethnic Filipinos in other locations - Northern California, New York, New Jersey, Connecticut, Washington, Oregon, Texas, Illinois, Indiana, Virginia, Maryland, Washington D.C., West Virginia, Tennessee, Arizona, Nevada, Georgia, New England states, Mid-West states, Toronto, Vancouver, Ireland, England, France, Tokyo-Japan, Hong kong, Taiwan, the Middle East, Philippines, and others.

Questions

1) In this round, what else did we miss that should be added to the list in this book?
2) For those Filipinos or ethnic Filipinos in other locations (Northern California, New York, New Jersey, Connecticut, Washington, Oregon, Texas, Illinois, Indiana, Virginia, Maryland, Washington D.C., West Virginia, Tennessee, Arizona, Nevada, Georgia, New England states, Mid-West states, Toronto, Vancouver, Ireland, England, France, Tokyo-Japan, Hong kong, Taiwan, the Middle East, Philippines, and others), what items in the book apply to you? We request "best practices" inputs and guidance from these locations.

Attributes of the Diaspora

Based on the research samples, there are at least 3 distinct groups: "Transplants" (arrived as adults); "Next Generations" (born here or arrived as toddlers); and, "Hybrids". Please note that the forward-looking, experienced and proficient leaders and constituents with corporate and mainstream backgrounds are mostly not participating in the organizations that we sampled.

"Transplants"

1) Excellent work ethics. In a scale of 0 to 10, 0 being the lowest and 10 the highest, work ethic is 9-10
2) There is no concept of National Identity or loyalty. They think of themselves as Ilocano, or Ilongo, or Pampageno, or Tagalog, or Visayan, etc.
3) Loyalty is with the family and region. They are predisposed to voting by region and not on merit or issues
4) Compared with other Diasporas, does not put emphasis on advanced degrees or training
5) Balat sibuyas mentality
6) Crab mentality
7) Libre mentality
8) King in a small island rather than a stakeholder in a bigger community mentality
9) Ningas kugon mentality
10) It is not my idea mentality

11) Self-denial mentality
12) Lack of trust
13) Suspicion of government
14) Lack of tolerance
15) Most leaders and constituents are not exposed to the "best practices" or "best of all world models" in other Diasporas and the mainstream
16) Consistently late in meetings
17) Given the opportunity to speak in meetings, there is tendency to take over the meeting
18) During meetings, the tendency to keep raising motions that have already been closed
19) Their meetings are usually 4-6 hours long, and in some cases without covering the announced agenda
20) Minimal standardization/discipline
21) Fond of social and cultural events but not activities that empowers and uplifts the community
22) Management by symbolism - decrees, picture taking, name dropping, awards
23) Connected to the homeland

"Next Generations" (those who are born or grew up in the U.S. since toddlers)

1) Compared to the "Transplants", they have moderate work ethics
2) In terms of National Identity, most think of themselves as Asian-Americans and not as Fil-Ams
3) Compared with other Diasporas, do not put emphasis on advanced degrees or training
4) Next generations are not region oriented, but are insular in perspective. They do not reach out to other communities at a level of other more successful Diasporas
5) "Barkada culture" while good in the social and cultural settings, it is a deterrent in professional advancement, business and political empowerment
6) Fond of social and cultural events but not activities that empowers and uplifts the community
7) Balat sibuyas mentality
8) Most leaders and constituents are not exposed to the "best practices" or "best of all world models" in other Diasporas and the mainstream
9) Understand and appreciate standardization and discipline but unable to take it to the next levels
10) Equipped for "baby step" improvements but not structural

improvements
11) Show some level of alienation from the "Transplants"
12) Detached from the Diaspora
13) Detached from the motherland

"Hybrids"

A mixture of the "Transplants" and "Next Generations"

Additional References

http://www.lulu.com/shop/david-paraiso/growing-up-and-parenting-two-score-and-four-years-ago/paperback/product-21269518.html

http://www.lulu.com/spotlight/DavidParaiso

Glossary and Terms

1) Balat Sibuyas – thin skin. This refers to operating within one's level of comfort only. The person with this mentality takes criticism or opinions from other people personally
2) Barkada culture - hanging out with friends
3) Corporate – mainstream; trade and commerce
4) Iberian and Middle East roots – a good number of Filipino cultural behavior have Spanish and Middle East roots
5) Invisible – marginalized
6) It is not my idea mentality – tendency to squash an idea or project because it did not come from the objector
7) Libre mentality - wants things but does not want to pay for it, like membership fee
8) Next Generations – are Filipinos who grew up here in the United States, or came here as toddlers
9) Ningas kugon – start something without completing it
10) Transplants – are Filipinos who came to the United States as adults.

Attachment A – Gaps with Other Diasporas

In the recent 40 years, The Fil-Am Diaspora community in Southern California has been losing ground to the other Diasporas – in politics, trade and commerce, choicest jobs and professional careers, and other types of empowerment.

At the person to person and family to family level – the Fi-Am Diaspora is competitive. But when it comes to across families, regions and national levels – we are not competitive.

Filipino Diaspora

> http://en.wikipedia.org/wiki/Filipino_American
>
> Total population
>
>> 3,416,840 - 4.5 million including multiracial Filipinos
>> 1.1% of the U.S. population (2010)
>
> Regions with significant populations
>
>> California (1,474,707), Hawaii (342,095), Illinois (139,090), Texas (137,713), Washington (137,083), New Jersey (126,793), New York (126,129), Nevada (123,891), Florida (122,691), Virginia (90,493), Maryland (56,909), Arizona (53,067)
>
> Languages
>
>> American English, Philippine English, Filipino, Tagalog, Cebuano, Ilocano, Ilongo, Bicolano, Waray, Kapampangan, Pangasinan, and others
>
> Religion
>
>> 65% Roman Catholicism, 21% Protestantism, 8% Irreligion, 1% Buddhism

Chinese Diaspora

http://en.wikipedia.org/wiki/Chinese_American

Total population

>3,794,673
>1.2% of the U.S. population (2010)

Regions with significant populations

>New York City, San Francisco, Los Angeles, Boston, Washington D.C., Chicago, Philadelphia, Seattle, Houston

Languages

>Predominantly English, varieties of Chinese:
>Mandarin Chinese (Standard Chinese), Yue Chinese (Cantonese, Taishanese), Min Chinese (Min Dong, Min Nan), Hakka, Wu Chinese (Taihu Wu, Oujiang Wu), and Minority Uyghur

Religion

>Unaffiliated, Protestantism, Buddhism, Catholicism

Related ethnic groups

>Hong Kong Americans, Taiwanese Americans
>Overseas Chinese

Vietnamese Diaspora

http://en.wikipedia.org/wiki/Vietnamese_American

Total population

>1,737,433 including those with partial ancestry
>0.6% of the US population (2010)

Regions with significant populations

>Southern California San Jose Houston Dallas Seattle Northern Virginia others

Languages

    Vietnamese, American English

Religion

    43% Buddhism, 30% Roman Catholicism
    20% unaffiliated, 6% Protestantism (2012)

Related ethnic groups

    Vietnamese people, Overseas Vietnamese, Vietnamese Canadians, Southeast Asian Americans, Asian Americans

Korean Diaspora

http://en.wikipedia.org/wiki/Korean_American

Total population

    1,706,822
    0.6% of the US population (2010)

Regions with significant populations

    Los Angeles metropolitan area, New York City metropolitan area, Washington, D.C. metropolitan area, and other major American metropolitan areas

Languages

    English, Korean

Religion

    61% Protestantism, 23% Unaffiliated,
    10% Roman Catholicism, 6% Buddhism

Japanese Diaspora

http://en.wikipedia.org/wiki/Japanese_American

Total population

> 763,325 alone, 0.2% of U.S. population
> 1,304,286 including partial ancestry, 0.4% (2010 Census)

Regions with significant populations

> Hawaii, the West Coast, and the Northeast

Languages

> American English and Japanese

Religion

> 32% Unaffiliated, 33% Protestantism, 25% Buddhism, 4% Catholicism, 4% Shinto (2012)

Armenian Diaspora

http://en.wikipedia.org/wiki/Armenian_American

Total population

> 483,366 (2011 ACS) — 1,500,000 (est.)
> 0.15%-0.5% of the US population

Regions with significant populations

> Greater Los Angeles Area • Northeastern urban areas

Languages

> Armenian • American English

Religion

> Predominantly Armenian Apostolic
> Minorities: Armenian Catholic and Armenian Evangelical

Iranian Diaspora

http://en.wikipedia.org/wiki/Iranian_American

Total population

448,722 (2010 ACS)

Regions with significant populations

California, New York, Texas, Maryland, Virginia, Washington DC.

Languages

American English, Persian and minority languages (see Languages of Iran)

Religion

Majority of Agnosticism, Atheism, Irreligion
Islam, Bahá'í Faith, Christianity, Judaism, Zoroastrianism

Indian Diaspora

http://en.wikipedia.org/wiki/Indian_American

Total population

3,183,063
1.0% of the U.S. population (2010)

Regions with significant populations

New Jersey, New York City, Atlanta, Raleigh-Durham, Baltimore-Washington, Boston, Chicago, Dallas, Houston, Los Angeles, Philadelphia, San Francisco Bay Area

Languages

American English, Hindi, Gujarati, other Indian languages

Religion

51% Hinduism, 23% Christianity, 10% Islam, 5% Unaffiliated, 5% Sikhism, 2% Jainism (2012)

Related ethnic groups

Indo-Canadians
NRI

Other Diasporas

http://en.wikipedia.org/wiki/List_of_diasporas

Attachment B – Medical Practice

Our data suggest that there are at least 25,000 board certified physicians and 200,000 nurses trained in the Philippines still practicing in the United States. Despite these numbers, the Fil-Am Diaspora has nothing close to the achievements of the Chinese, Hispanic, Korean and other communities. The Hispanics and Chinese have their own HMOs, hospitals and chains of medical facilities in the U.S. with links to their country of origin.

We were unable to trace any significant coalescing of various Fil-Am physicians or nurses at a level which is the norm in other Diasporas except during the "Desperate Housewives" episode which is temporary.

In 2006-2007, I was approached by a company which operates a chain of hospitals and clinics across the U.S. They are interested in investing in the Philippines, looking for a Fil-Am group of at least 200 physicians across specialties that can match $200 million in investment in 2 years. My research yielded the following: (1) the assets of known and active Fil-Am physicians practicing in the U.S., could easily raise the $200 million, or more; (2) however, most of them cannot work together under one umbrella. This company's first choice is the Philippines but because of the situation, they ended up reaching out to the Thais, Taiwanese and Indians. The mentality of being a king in a small island rather than a stakeholder in a bigger community is definitely hurting the Diaspora. In the recent 30 years, this is one of the many opportunities that I came across here in the U.S. that did not reach the 2nd base at all.

Within the state of California, we were unable to trace any Fil-Am medical group with meaningful and sustained outreach and linkages to federal, state, county and city elected officials. This means that most of the tax dollars and other resources go to other communities. Through inside contacts we know that there is an abundance of grant funds and political appointments in other communities.

A microcosm of a fragmented Diaspora is in the induction of officers of each medical alumni group – U.P., UST, UE, FEU, MCU and others. Instead of merging the induction into 1 event, one has to attend each event and pay at least $80 per event – that is $400 for 5 medical alumni groups that will take all night for each event.

References:

Obamacare Thrives In San Francisco's Chinatown

http://www.npr.org/blogs/health/2014/02/06/271121463/obamacare-thrives-in-san-francisco-s-chinatown

Chinese Community Health Plan

http://www.cahba.com/covered-california/chinese-community-health-plan.htm

https://www.cchphmo.com/

Chinese Community Health Plan (CCHP) was formed in 1986 as an alternative HMO for patients served by the Chinese Hospital Health System. The Health System was created more than a century ago to serve Chinese-Americans who were often excluded from mainstream healthcare. Today, CCHP continues to provide culturally competent care and is available to those who are employed and/or reside in San Francisco and Northern San Mateo Counties. CCHP serves Rating Regions 4 (San Francisco), 8 (San Mateo)

CCHP and its Integrated Health System has a history of participating in programs that benefit the Chinese community members that often have difficulty to access quality and affordable healthcare coverage.

The CCHP Network includes 9 hospitals and 315 doctors.

Molina Healthcare

http://www.molinahealthcare.com/en-us/Pages/home.aspx

http://www.cahba.com/california-health-insurance/molina-healthcare.htm

Molina Healthcare began in1980 as a single clinic providing care for low income individuals. Molina has since grown into a national managed care organization. Molina serves 5 rating regions in Covered California: Region 3 (Sacramento, Placer, El Dorado, Yolo), Region 15 (LA north), Region 16 (LA south), Region 17 (San Bernardino, Riverside), and Region19 (San Diego).

The Molina Network includes 29 hospitals and 4,568 doctors.

Attachment D – Music

For a list of these musical links, please send an email request to:

    Neanderthal.Conundrum@gmail.com

Bayan Ko – Freddie Aguilar, Lea Salonga, Mabuhay Singers

    http://www.youtube.com/watch?v=OtLWCY8O0us
    http://www.youtube.com/watch?v=xehDSjqac-k
    http://www.youtube.com/watch?v=4hWoutgPS4g
    http://en.wikipedia.org/wiki/Bayan_Ko

Mabuhay Singers - Sampaguita

    http://www.youtube.com/watch?v=4hWoutgPS4g

Anak Dalita / Pakiusap

    http://www.youtube.com/watch?v=k19rDndamuM

Mutya ng Pasig - Conching Rosal

    http://www.youtube.com/watch?v=wF6-i-ROnXU

Kundiman Art Song: Bituing Marikit - Conching Rosal

    http://www.youtube.com/watch?v=_JQxk8U7R0k

Kundiman ng Magandang Diwata - Conching Rosal

    http://www.youtube.com/watch?v=7zREIgy6yZM

Ang Maya - Conching Rosal

    http://www.youtube.com/watch?v=ENHl2jfEWfA

Sa Libis Ng Nayon (Balitaw) - Sylvia La Torre

http://www.youtube.com/watch?v=Tcb5GqznMXw

Pakiusap - Sylvia La Torre

http://www.youtube.com/watch?v=fiNjvB1M7_c

Ibong Sawi - Sylvia La Torre

http://www.youtube.com/watch?v=q94LxZ9y0To

Nasaan Ka Irog - Sylvia La Torre

http://www.youtube.com/watch?v=KlssZs-heXA

Babalik ka Rin - Sylvia La Torre

http://www.youtube.com/watch?v=Cxhig6a6Shc

Ang Dalagang Pilipina - Ruben Tagalog

http://www.youtube.com/watch?v=QCgWo9B4-4I

Maalaala Mo Kaya - Pilita Corrales

http://www.youtube.com/watch?v=j_6I0rDsLAE

Lumang Simbahan - Larry Miranda

http://www.youtube.com/watch?v=WXrv0zRzmm0

Dahil Sa'yo - Diomedes Maturan

http://www.youtube.com/watch?v=Nf_Td0EoT9U

Bulong-Bulungan - Diomedes Maturan

http://www.youtube.com/watch?v=-KGsS3591Oc

Buhat - Diomedes Maturan

http://www.youtube.com/watch?v=iKkCTRx4qHI

Paraluman - Ruben Tagalog

http://www.youtube.com/watch?v=IjS_S_sHsbs

Saan Ka Man Naroroon - Ric Manrique Jr.

http://www.youtube.com/watch?v=ALGWZAR_9I0

Salamat Sa Ala-ala - Cenon Lagman

http://www.youtube.com/watch?v=P8pJvwhJZ58

Ikaw - Ric Manrique Jr

http://www.youtube.com/watch?v=7m9siyhddNk

Saan Ka Man Naroroon - Ric Manrique Jr.

http://www.youtube.com/watch?v=ALGWZAR_9I0&list=RDl9kUmZ5kQGQ

Sapagkat Kami ay Tao Lamang - Ric Manrique Jr

http://www.youtube.com/watch?v=86dYi9bf5y8&list=RDl9kUmZ5kQGQ

Tanging Diyos Lamang Ang Nakakaalam - Ric Manrique Jr.

http://www.youtube.com/watch?v=l9kUmZ5kQGQ

Ang Tapis Mo Inday - Ruben Tagalog

http://www.youtube.com/watch?v=FVzu9VaF1Wc

O Ilaw - Ruben Tagalog

http://www.youtube.com/watch?v=NYueJU0Ufws

Mabuhay Singers - Perlas Ng Silangan

http://www.youtube.com/watch?v=Qgx1pSkFR5s

Tagalog Songs

http://www.youtube.com/watch?v=_qqBGzrMY7s

www.ingramcontent.com/pod-product-compliance
Lightning Source LLC
Chambersburg PA
CBHW031436040426
42444CB00006B/839